Making Marriage Last

John and Brandi Smith

Table of Contents

Introduction

Introduction

It is our heartfelt prayer that the Holy Spirit will use this book to help your marriage. Even with the best of intentions we are guilty of neglecting our marriages. Isn't it strange that we take the most precious things in our lives for granted? We work extremely diligent for things that don't matter and slack on the things that do. Marriage can so easily be neglected because we assume that is should naturally take care of itself. The truth of the matter is that marriage requires a plan of action if it is going to thrive. Marriage takes work and attention to produce the fruit we hope for. When people would ask how our marriage was going, I would respond with: "it takes a lot of work." We have discovered that a marriage that lasts a lifetime doesn't just happen. Two people took the steps and made the effort to make marriage last. God bless you.

Chapter 1

Walking with God - Faith

"And Enoch walked with God and he was not, for God took him."
(Genesis 2:24)

"But without faith it is impossible to please Him; for he that cometh to God must believe that He is and that He is a rewarder of them that diligently seek Him." (Hebrews 11:6)

There are many people today if asked the question, "Are you saved?" They would give a definite 'Yes'". If you were to ask them if they know God, they would more than likely say, "I guess so". But to ask someone if they are walking with God is a much more difficult question to answer. It is a bold statement to say, "I walk with God". It is one thing to say, "I am saved", but it is another to say, "I walk with God." It is one thing to say that I know who the President is; it is another to say "I know the President", but it is altogether different to say that "I walk with or work with the President". What does it mean to walk with God?

⁵ This then is the message which we have heard of him, and declare unto you, that God is light, and in him is no darkness at all.

⁶ If we say that we have fellowship with him, and walk in darkness, we lie, and do not the truth:

⁷ But if we walk in the light, as he is in the light, we have fellowship one with another, and the blood of Jesus Christ his Son cleanseth us from all sin.

⁸ If we say that we have no sin, we deceive ourselves, and the truth is not in us.

⁹ If we confess our sins, he is faithful and just to forgive us our sins, and to cleanse us from all unrighteousness. (1 John 1:5-9)

We will look at two results of walking with God. The most important foundation to marriage is your walk with God. Your relationship with

God must be right if your marriage relationship is going to be right. Our walk with God is individual and personal. My wife cannot walk with God for me and I cannot walk with God for her. We each must have a personal relationship with God.

The first benefit that flows from walking with God is:

I.   Fellowship with God

> *"But if we walk in the light, as he is in the light, we have fellowship one with another…"*(1 John 1:7a)

Fellowship with God is exercised through prayer and bible study. These two actions engage God and allow Him to engage us on a personal level. Christian service and activity should never be mistaken for fellowship with God. It is possible that we can serve God without knowing God. Apart from prayer and bible study we can't have true total fellowship with God. Reading the Bible allows the Holy Spirit to reveal God to us and prayer is how we communicate with the God we learn about. A person can be saved but not be growing in grace or in the knowledge of God (2 Peter 3:18). The scripture is where I learn who God is and consequently who I became when I was baptized into Christ.

When a husband and wife are in personal fellowship with God through Bible and prayer there are two blessings that follow. These two blessings are crucial in a marriage that will last a lifetime. The first blessing from fellowship with God is **right desires**. Right desires come from God. The Bible teaches in Psalms 37:4 *"Delight thyself also in the LORD: and he shall give thee the desires of thine heart."* Making fellowship with God a priority will allow God to produce in us His desires. When a Christian has a life that is yielded to God and is in submission to His will there will be a fellowship that produces right desires (John 15). These desires will always be godly desires. As we fellowship with God we begin to understand that we are like him (I John 4:17). Apart from Christ our desires are selfish and ungodly. (John 15:5)

"But we are all as an unclean thing, and all our righteousness are as filthy rags; and we all fade as a leaf; and our iniquities, like the wind, have taken us away." (Isaiah 64:6)

When we follow our own desires (James 1:14), we can hurt and wound our marriage and the people we love. God is a good God and He is holy and everything that He does is always right. Therefore, the desires that He will create in our hearts will always be good, right and holy. It is important in relationships to have the right desires. When a husband and wife are full of God's desires then they will consider each other and care for each other like God cares for us.

Fellowship with God will also produce in us **right direction**. There are many choices in life. Where to live? Where to work? Where to attend church? Who to marry? How many children to have? Only to name a few. With so many good choices the only way for a husband and wife to travel in the same direction is for both of them to be led by God. The Bible teaches:

"In all thy ways acknowledge Him and He shall direct thy paths." (Proverbs 3:6)

As we delight in God, He deposits in us His desires and as we look to Him, He will give us His direction. When a husband and a wife ask God for direction, He will always lead them in the <u>same direction</u>.

Discussion Questions:

1. What are some desires you have right now?
2. Which desires are from the Lord?
3. Which desires are from your flesh?

There is a great danger in going our own way. When a husband and wife go their own direction, it may not be the same direction. For marriage to work in harmony as God intends both husband and wife will need to be walking in the same direction. The Bible teaches:

"Can two walk together, except they be agreed?" (Amos 3:3)

For husband and wife to walk together they must both walk with God. As humans we can fall into the idea of thinking that we know best. The reality is we do not know best. We need for God to give us moment by moment direction.

"There is a way that seemeth right unto a man, but the end thereof are the ways of death." (Proverbs 16:25)

As the Christian learns that it is God in them and what it means to walk in Him, God will give that person right direction in their life. (2 Corinthians 6:16) This is often difficult for most people because it requires us to exercise something called faith. Many times, God given, God inspired direction will go against all common sense. It is at this point we must move forward by faith. There are three steps to faith that pleases God.

"By faith Noah, being warned of God of things not seen as yet, moved with fear, prepared an ark to the saving of his house; by the which He condemned the world, and became heir of the righteousness which is by faith." (Hebrews 11:7)

1. Faith Acknowledging (Hebrews 11:7a)

A husband and wife must first begin by acknowledging God in all of their ways. This means that we must include God in every decision. We must ask God to give us a biblical world view.

2. Faith Agreeing (Hebrews 11:7b)

This step requires the husband and wife to lay aside what they think and agree with what God says.

3. Faith Acting (Hebrews 11:7c)

This is when many husbands and wives can go wrong. If you stop short of complete obedience to what God has said, then you cease to be waking with God. To walk in God's direction means to walk in obedience to what God has revealed.

Many people don't live by faith because of the risk involved. You may be thinking, "Risk? What risk?" There is always a risk when walking by faith. The risk is-did God really say it? Did we really hear from God? We all would confess that we trust God. Our trouble is we don't trust ourselves. Many times, we don't act on what we believe God is saying to us because we are fearful of not knowing what will come next. When Christian men and women take one step by faith that one step leads to another step. Over time we find that our life is made up of a series of steps that we have been taking by faith. We heard a word from God. He gave us a desire and direction and we acted on what we believed that He was saying to us. Suddenly we realize how much we are dependent upon God. We find that we need Him more than we ever have needed Him before because we are no longer living our own life, walking our own direction or fulfilling our own desires. Instead, we are walking in tune with a living God. If faith does not result in obedience, then our faith is dead.

"For as the body without the spirit is dead, so faith without works is dead also," (James 2:26)

When a husband lives by faith and obedience to what God reveals to him and when a wife lives by faith and obedience to what God reveals to her, there is no way they can be divided. This is not to say that they will not disagree or argue, however they will be able to experience and live in unity, love, honor, and respect with and for each other.

"...every city or house divided against itself shall not stand." (Matthew 12:25)

Marriage is when two individual people (male and female) are joined together.

> *"Therefore shall a man leave his father and his mother, and shall cleave unto his wife: and they shall be one flesh."* (Genesis 2:24)

God never intended for a husband and wife to be divided. Therefore, if they find themselves divided then they are not walking with God in truth. The foundation of marriage is recognizing individual abiding fellowship with God. Without this there is nothing to build upon. There will be no boundaries and no accountability.

Discussion Questions:

1. How does walking with God benefit our marriage?

2. How does not walking with God affect our marriage?

Part 2 – Walking with God

The second benefit that flows from walking with God is:

II.   Forgiveness by God (I John 1:7b)

When a husband and wife walk with God in intimate fellowship God reveals their sin to them. Remember that God does not reveal sin to you so that He can punish you. He does it so that you can confess and forsake sin and He can cleanse and forgive you. A guilty conscience will hinder our walk with God. If our conscience is in bondage to self-condemnation the result is that we hide from God. This is exactly what happened to Adam in the garden (Genesis 3:9). He sinned against God by eating the forbidden fruit. When he ate the fruit, his eyes were opened, and he knew that he was naked. When he heard God walking in the garden he went and hid himself from God. Make a special note here, God is the one who showed up for fellowship and Adam was the one hiding. Sin in the Christians life will make the conscience guilty and we break fellowship with God. A husband or wife should never run *from* God with sin, instead they should run *to* God with their sin.

a. Light Reveals Sin (I John 1:9a)
"God is light and in Him is no darkness at all…" Light is used for many things. It is used for giving direction and helping us to see. By nature, light swallows up darkness. Darkness is the absence of light. But we are never absent from light because God is light, and God lives in us. But sin attempts to deceive us and creep into our lives. As a christian walks with God not only does he have fellowship with God, he also has the forgiveness of his sin. God is light and He reveals to us when darkness attempts to take us captive. It is impossible to walk with God and not be keenly aware of sin attacks. (We must keep in focus that sin no longer lives in us as it once did before our second

birth. It is now only an outside attack against the body and soul attempting to deceive us and condemn us.) By nature, God is light, and God is in us, consequently we contain the light. Therefore, He is always revealing and exposing sin attacks. Light reveals sin. David prayed,

"Search me, O God, and know my heart: try me, and know my thoughts,
And see if [there be any] wicked way in me, and lead me in the way everlasting". Psalm 139:23-24

It is God who must search us for sin. When we search ourselves we don't see clearly. We need the light that comes from fellowship with God to show us. Do not fall into the wrong thinking that you must be without sin before you come to God. There is none who are without sin. We must come into the light and let God expose which sins are in our lives.

b. Light Leads to Repentance (I John 1:9b)

Our desires are His desires because we have fellowship with Him. Because we are in fellowship with God, as we already read, we desire what He desires.

"But as he which hath called you is holy, so be ye holy in all manner of conversation: Because it is written, be ye holy, for I am holy." (1 Peter 1:15-16)

God will expose when sin attacks us. As we walk with God it will become clear the times we have yielded to sin. Remember that temptation is not sin. It is only when lust is conceived is sin produced (James 1:15). As we fellowship with God through the Bible and in prayer our desire will be forgiveness and cleansing. This desire will lead to confession and repentance. Forgiveness is as quick as the committing of sin when we confess. Confess means that we agree with what God reveals to us in the light of His presence.

> *"He that covereth his sins shall not prosper: but whoso confesseth and forsaketh them shall have mercy."* (Proverbs 28:13)

As a husband and wife, we must be careful to confess our sins to God. If we don't confess to God, then we will not prosper. Our walk with God comes to a screaming halt as soon as we cover and conceal sins. Covering sin will be like a cancer eating away and destroying marriage. Sin is the enemy. Don't let the enemy live tucked away in secret. Confess in the light and be forgiven and cleansed. Your marriage depends on it.

> *"For I will be merciful to their unrighteousness and their sins and their iniquities will I remember no more."* (Hebrews 8:12)

God longs to give you mercy. Mercy is not getting what you deserve. We deserve judgment for sin, but God gives us mercy. The only way that God can give mercy to you and me is because of what Jesus accomplished on the cross.

How does being forgiven of sins benefit our marriage?

1. Humility

It takes humility to confess sin to your spouse. Humility is always good for marriage. Humility is a building block in a strong marriage. Pride will destroy a marriage. Sin has a way of humbling us. We realize that we are not perfect and that we are in need of grace. This will help us remember that our spouse is in need of grace as well.

2. Transparency

Every marriage requires complete transparency to thrive and grow. It takes openness and honesty to have a good marriage. Don't hide anything. Transparency is what makes trust possible. We all know that without trust we can't have meaningful relationships.

3. Accountability

When we live without accountability, we become more and more selfish and empowered. Selfishness will hurt relationships. Once you confess your sins, your spouse can help hold you accountable.

4. Merciful

When we recognize the mercy that the Lord has shown us for our sins, it allows us to give mercy to our spouse. I am sure you have realized by now that you did not marry a perfect flawless person. They are going to fail. They need mercy from you. Forgiveness is crucial in a healthy marriage. Every marriage is built on forgiveness. A strong marriage is not the absence of hurt it is being merciful to those who hurt us.

How does covering our sin affect our marriage?

> *He who conceals* (hides, buries, keeps) *his transgressions* (sin, rebellion, disobedience)*, will not prosper* (be fruitful, be blessed, move forward, live in victory)

> An example of a man who concealed his sin is Achan:

>> *"So Achan answered Joshua and said truly I have sinned against the Lord, the God of Israel, and this is what I did: when I saw among the spoil a beautiful mantle from Shinar and two hundred shekels of silver and a bar of gold fifty shekels in weight, then I coveted them and took them; and behold, they are concealed in the earth inside my tent with the silver underneath it."* (Joshua 7:20-21)

Three things concealed sin does.

I.   Concealed sin hurts others

> *"The men of Ai smote of them about thirty and six men: for they chased them from before the gate even unto Sheb'-a-rim, and smote them in the going down: wherefore the hearts of the people melted, and became as water."* (Joshua 7:5)

II.   Concealed sin cripples us before our enemy

> *"Therefore the children of Israel could not stand before their enemies, but turned their backs before their enemies, because they were accursed...."* (Joshua 7:12)

III.   Concealed sin hurts our family

> *"And Joshua and all Israel with him, took Achan the son of Zerah, and the silver, and the garment, and the wedge of gold, and his sons, and his daughters, and his oxen, and his asses, and his sheep, and his tent, and all that he had and they brought them unto the valley of Achor... And all Israel stoned him with stones and burned them with fire after they had stoned them with stones."* (Joshua 7:24-25)

Our personal walk with God as a husband and wife is the foundation of our marriage. Without this we will not have a marriage that will last and honor God. There is no such thing as a perfect marriage, but marriage can be done perfectly when both walk with God.

What are some practical steps we all can take to walk with God?

    I.   Individually
        a. Daily prayer
        b. Daily Bible Reading
    II.   As a couple
        a. Pray together daily
        b. Read the Scripture together daily
        c. Attend church regularly together
        d. Serve the Lord in some way together

> Application: For the next seven days you and your spouse wake up 30 minutes earlier each morning. (Or do this right before you go to bed). Spend this time together. Men lead in prayer. Pray for yourself and your wife and ask God to give you both direction and desire. Ask him to give you both understanding of the scripture and ask him to fill both you and your wife with the Holy Spirit. This next week we will be reading through the book of Ephesians together. Husband read out loud the first three verses, then let your wife read the next three and do this until you reach the end of the chapter. Then share with one another if there was anything that stood out to you. Lastly, husbands close your time together with a word of prayer.

Chapter 2

God's Purposes in Marriage

Discussion Questions:

1. What do you think God's purpose in marriage is?

2. Why do you think most people get married?

The most common reasons for marriage that we hear people say are; "She makes me happy." "He completes me." "We love each other." The trouble with these statements comes when we consider the opposite questions. "What are you going to do when she doesn't make you happy?" "What will you do when he no longer completes you?" "What will happen when you no longer think or feel you love each other?" Many occasions couples look at me as if to ask, "Is that possible?"

Many people who get married- both young and old- sometimes have the wrong perception of marriage. **A wrong perception of marriage creates the wrong expectations in marriage.** If we were to take a survey among married couples just in this community and ask them if their marriage is what they thought that it was going to be, most would say that it's not. Some would say that it is better than they imagined while others would say that it is worse than they could have imagined. A large majority of marriages are falling apart and tearing at the seams. Hearts are filled with bitterness, unforgiveness, a sense of betrayal, feelings of rejection, anger, resentment, jealously and every other kind of unpleasantness you can name. Why is this? I would suggest to you it is because most do not understand God's ultimate purpose in marriage.

When someone enters into marriage with the focus of getting their own needs met the foundation is weak. When our spouse fails to meet all of our expectations, we grow bitter and resentful toward our spouse. Many people see marriage as a trap they have gotten caught in with no chance of escape, and the bait that took them was the false understanding of happily ever after.

Before I got married men would say to me that I better run while I still have the chance. Men would joke about how bad their marriage was. As time passes an attitude can develop of, "Oh well, I guess this is the way it will always be." Individuals or couples give up and quit on their spouse. They are still married in the legal sense and they share the same roof. They have sex every now and then but their heart and soul are far away from each other. Now their life is reduced to one of survival. They go to work, pay bills, eat, sleep, get up and do it all over again. The reason could be because they have viewed marriage all wrong and not as God intends for it to be.

We are going to look in the scriptures at five of God's purposes in marriage. We will look at four in brief and spend most of our time on the fifth purpose. If we can get a grip on the fifth purpose it can transform a good marriage into a better marriage and a struggling marriage into a thriving marriage.

5 Purposes in Marriage

I.   Help Meet

> *"And the Lord God said, it is not good that the man should be alone; I will make him an help meet for him..."* (Genesis 2:18, 21-25)

A help meet is a suitable helper. God created Eve to help Adam with his God given responsibilities.

II.   Reproduction

> *"So God created man in his own image, in the image of God He created him; male and female created he them. And God blessed them, and God said unto them, Be fruitful, and multiply, and replenish the earth, and subdue it..."* (Genesis 1:27-28)

Marriage is the relationship through which God has chosen to procreate.

III.   Sexual Pleasure & Fulfillment

"Let the husband render unto the wife due benevolence: and likewise also the wife unto the husband...Defraud ye not one the other, except it be with consent for a time, that ye may give yourselves to fasting and prayer; and come together again, that Satan tempt you not for your incontinency (lack of self-control*)."* (1Corinthians 7:3-5)

Marriage is the relationship of sexual expression. Sexual drive is a gift from God and is honorable in the confines of the marriage bed alone. Don't feel guilty to enjoy sex in marriage. God blessed you and your spouse with this gift to freely enjoy.

IV.   Picture of Christ and the Church

"For this cause shall a man leave his father and mother, and shall be joined unto his wife, and they two shall be one flesh. This is a great mystery: but I speak concerning Christ and the church." (Ephesians 5:31-32)

The marriage relationship is between one man and one woman freely given to each other until death. The husband is to be the picture of Christ and His sacrificial love for the church. The husband is to love his wife as Christ loved the church and gave himself for her. The wife is the picture of the church and how the church is to follow and obey Christ.

V.   Conformity to Christ

a. Salvation
We know that the Scriptures teach us that God's will for mankind is their salvation.

"For this is good and acceptable in the sight of God our Savior; who will have all men to be saved, and to come unto the knowledge of the truth." (1 Timothy 2:3-4)

"The Lord is not slack concerning his promise, as some men count slackness; but is longsuffering to us-ward, not willing that any should perish, but that all should come to repentance." (2 Peter 3:9)

God desires for you to be saved. If you have not been saved God loves you. He proved His love for you by giving His Son Jesus to die for you. He was crucified, buried and resurrected. Trust Jesus today before it is everlasting too late.

b. Sanctification
God's purpose in salvation is that we be conformed into the image of His Son Jesus Christ.

"And we know that all things work together for good to them that love God, to them who are the called according to his purpose. For whom he did foreknow, he also did predestinate to be conformed to the image of his Son, that he might be the first born among many brethren." (Romans 8:28-29)

"All things": Not only the good things and the pleasant things but everything; the good, the bad, and the ugly. Everything is always at all times in every situation and every circumstance working together for our good. Notice that it does not say anything about our pleasure, our happiness, our joyfulness, our peacefulness, our contentment, or our satisfaction. Actually, it is important to consider what the good is that all things are working together for in our lives.

The good is our conformity to the image of His Son. What could be better in the life of a child of God? It is our conformity to Christ that all things are working together for. Take every event, every success, every failure, every argument, every outburst of anger, every mistake and put them all together and they are designed or allowed to fit together and produce results for your good- (conformity to Christ) never to destroy you. When we don't understand this principal in marriage, we can fall into the trap that I've called "the blame game".

God uses the marriage relationship to FORM Christ in us. **Marriage magnifies what is in our hearts**. God uses marriage to draw out what is in our hearts.

Let me try to use a personal example to illustrate this point. Before I met my wife Brandi, I was a single young man who had been saved in a miraculous way. My whole life had been changed in a moment. I read my Bible every morning, during lunch, and every night. I was never far from the Scriptures. I prayed, did ministry and sought the face of God. I would often pray that God would make me more like Jesus. I thought of myself as a good Christian. I thought I was selfless and sacrificial. I thought I knew how to love. I thought I had control over my temper. I thought that I was great at encouraging people. Then I met Brandi and by God's grace we married. I soon began to realize who I thought I was and who I really was, was not the same. I discovered that I was not as selfless and sacrificial as I had thought. Also, I realized that I did not have control of my temper. All of these awful things that I did not think existed in my life were suddenly there. At first, I began to blame Brandi. I believed that she was causing me to say the things that I said or act the way I was acting. I found myself making apologies that sounded like this, "I am sorry that I said that to you, but if you would not have done that, I would not have said it." Or, "I am sorry that I lost my temper with you but if you would have done this, I would not have gotten so angry." The truth is, that is not an apology. I was blaming her for my actions. I was blaming her, therefore I was not acknowledging or taking responsibility for my own behavior. It was never my fault. I blamed her for my actions.

Many of us blame our spouse for our behavior because we don't understand God's principle of our conformity to Christ in our marriage. Your spouse doesn't cause you to act the way you act or say the things you say. All of these things are *already* in your heart; God just uses your spouse to expose you to yourself. This is not to hurt us or destroy us or to make us look bad in front of our spouse. God's ultimate purpose in our lives is that we be conformed to the image of Christ. He gave us a spouse to help in this process.

There are three steps that must take place in a spouse's heart to be conformed into the image of Christ through their marriage:

I.   Realizing our Need for Conformity

     When God uses our spouse to reveal to us our need there are two ways we can respond:
1.   We can blame our spouse for our behavior
2.   We can take responsibility for our own actions

     You must wake up to the reality that you have not arrived. You are not perfect, you have flaws, you have issues, we all do. You have to realize your need.

II.   Confessing our Need for Conformity

     After we take responsibility for our actions then we must agree with God that we are still full of self and that we need to be changed.

     Confession means to **agree with God**.

III.   Praying for our Need for Conformity

     Once we have confessed to God that we are aware of our need to be changed then we humble ourselves and ask God to do only what He can do. It is only God who can change us. There is nothing that we can do except ask Him and trust in Him to do this.

The first step in being conformed into the image of Christ is realizing our need to be conformed. **God moves us to where he wants us by revealing to us where we are.** If we think we are doing well where we are there is not a desire or motivation to change. God uses our spouse to bring out the best in us and also the worst. Whoever you are around and toward your spouse is who you really are. We can put on a front all day at work and be cordial, patient and sweet. However, as soon as our spouse calls or comes home we become rude, irritable, frustrated, and sharp. Why is that? Because God uses marriage to reveal who we really are. Many resent their spouse because of this and can begin to think, "I would be happy if I wasn't married to her, she is the only person that causes me to act this way." "I would be much happier, but my husband always irritates me." Remember that you are who you are when you are with your spouse. We let our guard down. Your spouse can never make you behave or say things. Those things are in you. God wants to get them out.

If we understand the purpose of conformity in marriage, we can stop pointing our finger at our spouse and blaming them for our behavior. Instead, we can acknowledge that God loves us enough to develop our understanding of who Christ is in us through our most trusted ally, our spouse. Then we can confess to God what we see to be our tendencies and repent, when we fail, and trust Him to conform us into the image of His Son Jesus Christ.

Illustration:

A husband is very sensitive to be early for any meeting that he has. He believes that it shows respect for the person that he is to meet. He also believes that his punctuality gives him a reputation of being responsible. At the same time, his wife constantly is the source of his tardiness. She rarely gives herself enough time to get ready. She likes to be on time, but it just seems that she has a hard time getting things together. As usual, the husband is ready fifteen minutes before the appointed time to leave the house. As usual, his wife is running behind. He tells her from the front room that she has fifteen minutes. She tells him that she is trying but it took a little longer than she remembered to dry her hair. He huffs and mumbles a few words to himself and decides to sit down in his recliner. Seventeen minutes later she comes out of the backroom in a hurry with her shoes in her hands, her slip showing, and her makeup bag on her arm saying, "I'll just do my make up in the car". The husband is holding it together as best he can but on the inside he has had it. He is sharp with her and he shows it by walking ahead of her to the car. He cranks the car and puts on his seat belt. Then he watches her struggle carrying all of her stuff to the car. She fumbles around trying to open her own door and the husband is thinking, "Serves her right! She should have been on time! I'm not going to help her." She gets in the car and says, "By the way, I forgot to get gas on my way home this morning and we need to stop and get some". The husband finally has had all he can handle. He yells at her for being late. "You always do this! You know I like to be on time!" She responds, "I didn't mean to make us late." He says, "It doesn't matter if you meant to or not we're still late, now we are going to be later because you left the car on empty!" The wife replies, "I am sorry, I didn't mean to." "Yeah you are sorry, sorry at managing your time!" her husband says rudely. His wife then begins to cry and asks, "Why do you have to be so rude?" He gets mad that she accuses him of being rude and hits the steering wheel and says, "I wasn't like this until you made us late for our meeting. If you would have been on time we would have had a pleasant night. It's your fault."

Now what we have here is an example of a husband who doesn't see or understand what God is trying to teach him through his spouse's tardiness. He thinks it is her fault that he is behaving the way he is behaving. Yes, in reality she is late. But, for her husband to behave the way he does only reveals that he lacks self-control and that he lacks patience. **Many times we want God to change our spouse when in reality he is trying to change us**.

How would a patient man who has self-control have responded to his tardy wife?

Discussion Question

1. How can viewing your marriage in light of your conformity to Christ help you in your marriage?

Application
1. Pay attention to what rises up within you when there is
   conflict with your spouse.
2. Don't blame your spouse for your behavior.
3. Take full responsibility for your behavior.
4. Apologize to your spouse when you react in a way that is not
   Christ like.
5. Pray for God to help you respond more like Christ next time.

Remember there is a retest when you don't pass the first, second,
third, fourth, fifth, etc.

Homework:

For the next seven days continue to rise early or stay up late with
your spouse for prayer and Bible reading. This week read first Peter
and second Peter.

Chapter 3

Conflict Resolution - Humility

Is unresolved conflict ever biblical?

Problems in marriage don't work themselves out over time. Every problem must be given proper time and effort from both people to ensure closure. If there is not closure on both sides, then there is still a problem even though we may not be able to see it. When we avoid and ignore problems time has a way of helping us forget about them until the next conflict arises and we see that they are still there. We may think the unresolved problem is gone because it has not been brought up in awhile...but rest assured it is still there. It is somewhere under the surface waiting to rear its ugly head again. Our enemy, Satan, loves when couples leave unattended baggage lying around. Quite often it is simply the things that went unsaid. He is the master of magnification. He loves to bring things up in our minds and make them look a lot different than they really are. When unresolved problems and conflicts are left open ended "assumption" steps in and blows things out of proportion.

Often couples let small conflicts fall by the wayside and never completely deal with them. If we leave enough small things unattended, they can grow into big issues over time. Just because you have shrugged it off as no big deal doesn't mean your spouse has. This is why honest communication daily is vital to a marriage that will last. Every so often it is good to evaluate your marriage and make sure everything is out in the open.

Unresolved conflict always bears the fruit of bitterness and wrath. Conflict is defined by Noah Webster as a war of two or more opposing ideas, a clash or opposition. When there is conflict between husband and wife there is a war of ideas, there is a clash. In a conflict both parties believe that they are right. Whether they are right or wrong it doesn't matter-they still honestly believe themselves to be right. When a person thinks they are right they feel justified in defending or arguing their point. This is normal. Naturally, while supporting or arguing our position we are tearing down our spouse's position. This is why a conflict between a husband and wife can become heated and intense even over a small issue in life. It is easy to take things personal when someone is attacking what you think to be right and true. If conflict is not handled properly it can cause one or both people to feel disrespected and hurt by their spouse.

The Scripture teaches us the importance of resolving conflict. It also warns us of the consequences if we do not resolve conflict.

A. The Offended – "I am angry with someone"

"Be ye angry, and sin not: let not the sun go down upon your wrath: Neither give place to the devil." (Ephesians 4:26-27)

Here we have a situation of someone that has been offended by another person. Scripture justifies their anger. They are warned not to sin in their anger. There is a fine line not to cross and anger can easily turn into wrath if not properly handled and resolved. The bible instructs the offended party to seek to make things right for his own sake *(let not the sun go down upon your wrath)*. This is a command to go to the person who has offended you before the day is done and talk out what is in your heart so that you may let go of your wrath towards the person.

If we let the sun go down upon our wrath, we then are giving place to the devil. We are giving our adversary an opportunity to work in our hearts. He loves to pervert and twist our thoughts and emotions. Our thinking is the battle ground and if we have allowed unresolved conflict towards our spouse to dwell in our hearts the devil will use it to divide husband from wife and wife from husband. The devil already has plenty of ammunition to accuse us with. It is not wise to give him more.

Illustration: John accidentally shut the door on our babies' finger and Brandi was mad at him for doing so. Brandi said, "John I am mad at you for shutting little John's finger in the door. One third of his finger is dangling by a thread and now we have to go to the hospital and have emergency surgery to sew it back together. I'm afraid he will lose his finger." John replies, "I'm so sorry honey. You know I didn't mean to. I was helping our other son and didn't see him behind me." Brandi said, "Well, I forgive you then."

She forgave him so she would not become bitter at him later.

A. The Offender – "I have made someone angry"

"Therefore if thou bring thy gift before the alter, and there rememberest that thy brother hath aught against thee; leave there thy gift before the altar, and go thy way; first be reconciled to thy brother, and then come and offer thy gift." (Matthew 5:23-24)

If we remember that we have offended someone, and they have aught against us then we are commanded to go and make things right with them. The Scripture always points Christians to hate division and love reconciliation.

Notice in the Scriptures that the one who is offended is called upon by God to go make things right and also the one who has offended is called upon to go and make things right. It does not matter who has offended who, God just wants one of you to take the initiative to make things right. Humble yourself and bridge the gap. Your marriage is worth it. Your spouse is worth it. Your Savior is worthy of it.

Three ways **not** to handle Conflict

    I.   Intimidation

          This is usually what men do when there is conflict

          Example: Threatening, raising their voice, pressuring

    II.   Manipulation

This is usually what women do when there is conflict

Example: Crying, withholding sex, turning the tables

III. Avoidance

This is when no one wants to deal with it, and they try to ignore it

Two Major Hindrances to Conflict Resolution

I. Pride

    a. Keeps us from admitting we are wrong

        What is wrong with being wrong?
        Why do you insist on being right?

    b. Can cause us to hurt our spouse in pursuit of being right

II. Selfishness

    a. We want things done our way
    b. We put our interests above our spouse's

Three Steps to Conflict Resolution

I.   Someone has to **take initiative** (Ephesians 4:26-27; Matthew 5:23-24)

    a. Humble yourself
    b. Honor your spouse

    "Let nothing be done through strife and vainglory; but in lowliness of mind let each

esteem other better than themselves."
(Philippians 2:3)

Do not wait on your spouse to come to you. Go to them. It doesn't matter who is the culprit in the situation. Make the first move and see to it that you both find a resolution.

II.   **Talk it Out** – Remember you are on the same team

a.   What does God say about it?
b.   Honestly deal with it
c.   Stay on Subject

Do not bring up past conflicts and problems as weapons against your spouse. Allow your spouse to share how the feel. Be sure not to interrupt or make faces and use body language that makes them feel guilty for sharing.

III.   Work together to defeat what threatens your marriage. **Together fix it**.

a.   Come to a conclusion

If there is a difference of opinion and both believe that they are right in the decision, then they are to do what the scripture says in Ephesians 5:23:

"Therefore as the church is subject unto Christ, so let the wives be to their own husbands in everything."

This is not to be taken that the wife should not be heard and honored. There is nothing to say that the husband can't go with his wife on the decision. Sometimes there may be an immediate decision that needs to be made and the husband may need to make the call and take the burden of the decision upon himself to free his wife. If the conflict is life altering or complicated do not hesitate to see a Christian marriage counselor to help you come to a conclusion.

b. Ask for forgiveness

It is of utmost importance to use the words "Please forgive me." or "Will you forgive me?"

In our relationship with God the Father we are taught to pray, *"Father forgive us our sins..."* (Luke 11:4).

When these words are used there is resolve.

c. Give forgiveness

When our spouse asks for forgiveness for the wrong that they have done we are always to give it. It is very important to use the words "I forgive you." Never say, "It is no big deal." Or "Don't worry about it." It is a big deal and it needs to be dealt with properly. When we say the words "I forgive you", that is the end of the matter. Closure has come and now we can move forward in life together with no division.

"And if he trespass against thee seven times in a day, and seven times in a day turn again to thee, saying, I repent; thou shalt forgive him." (Luke 17:4)

The way to know that a conflict has been dealt with properly and completely is it will not be used at a later time as a weapon to hurt a spouse. There was a great conflict between God and man. In reality God did nothing wrong to provoke or give mankind reason for his disobedience and rejection of God. Mankind on its own rebelled against God and this brought about a great conflict. There was nothing that the guilty party could do in order to make things right with God. Therefore:

I. God took the initiative.

"For God so loved the world that he gave his only begotten Son, that whosoever believeth in him should not perish, but have eternal life." (John 3:16)

II. God humbled Himself.

"But made himself of no reputation, and took upon him the form of a servant, and was made in the likeness of men: And being found in fashion as a man, he humbled himself, and became obedient unto death, even the death of the cross." (Philippians 2:7-8)

III. God treated man as if it never happened.

"Therefore being justified by faith, we have peace with God through our Lord Jesus Christ:" (Romans 5:1)

Your spouse is not your enemy. Remind yourself of that and remind your spouse of that. You are a team. Come together and deal with the problem at hand. Find a Christ honoring solution. Be honest. Confess your part. Forgive when forgiveness is needed.

Homework

*Read Psalm 139
*Intentionally set aside time to talk with God and ask Him to show you if there is any resentment or bitterness in your heart toward your spouse.
*Be prepared with a pen and paper to write down what God shows you.
*Ask God to show you if there is something that you have done to cause your spouse to resent you or be bitter with you and write down anything God shows you.

"Search me, O God, and know my heart: try me, and know my thoughts: And see if there be any wicked way in me, and lead me in the way everlasting." (Psalm 139:23-24)

Chapter 4

God's Order – Husbands

Introduction: Order is good and needful. When something is out of order it cannot work properly. Its original design and purpose is hindered because one or more parts are not doing their part or specific role. Take a drink machine for example. If it has a sign on the front that says "Out of Order" you know you can't get a drink out of it. You cannot use it and it won't produce anything good until it is fixed.

In marriage God has designed and designated a certain order and roles that must not be out of order. When marriage is out of order, like a drink machine, it cannot work as it was desgined to work.

We know that the Bible gives clear instructions to the husband and wife. *"In the image of God created he him; male and female created he them."* (Genesis 1:27) In God's wisdom and understanding He has assigned specific tasks and responsibilities to each. It is God's desire that each of us fulfill our role in our marriage. **When we fulfill our role, God is glorified in our marriages.**

We can observe from the creation account in Genesis that God is a God of establishing order. *"And the earth was without form, and void; and darkness was upon the face of the deep. And the spirit of God moved upon the face of the waters."* (Genesis 1:2)

There was no order in the earth, but God established order. The animals brought forth animals after their own kind and plants after their own kind. The days and nights were set into place. Everything was put into order and was given its place in creation according to His purpose and design. We see order in the church and spiritual authority. When Paul writes to the Corinthian church, he reflects the heart and nature of God when he writes, *"Let all things be done decently and in order"* (1 Corinthians 14:40)

I.   His Role

God always has order and position of rank in His kingdom and it is no different in the family. God has placed the husband as the head of the wife and the spiritual head of the home. This comes with great responsibility and should be done with love.

"For the husband is the head of the wife, even as Christ is the head of the Church: and he is the saviour of the body...Husbands, love your wives, even as Christ also loved the Church, and he gave himself for it;" (Ephesians 5:23,25)

Often, I find it difficult to grasp exactly what the responsibility of the husband looks like. We know that we are to love our wife as Christ loved the church and gave himself for it, but what does that look like for a man to give his life for his wife? I have heard it said that the husband is to give up everything and anything that he wants in order to please and serve his wife; whenever she wants something he is to drop everything right then and there to go and serve her. Is that what we as husbands are to do? I have frustrated myself trying to understand what it means to love my wife and honor her. I am going to try and help us grasp what it is to look like through an illustration. This is not a "how to love your wife" lesson, but I pray that it will help us have a better understanding of what it means to love and lead our wives as God calls us to.

In Genesis 1:26 we see that God created man in His image and then placed him in the garden of Eden to have dominion over it. Adam was given dominion over the garden. He wasn't to dominate as if in a struggle or war but **to take responsibility for and to care for God's creation**.

"And the Lord God took the man, and put him into the Garden of Eden to dress it and to keep it."(Genesis 2:15)

The term dress means, "to serve, to be served, to work."

I find it interesting that it means to serve AND to be served. Service goes both ways. Each spouse should give 100 percent. The husband should not expect the wife to serve him and the wife should not expect the husband to serve her. They should both serve each other.

As Adam served the garden and worked the garden, he was in return served by the garden. The fruit of the garden was there for him to freely enjoy.

The term **keep** means, "tending or exercising great care over the garden, to guard".

As the keeper of the garden he was responsible to tend to it, to pay attention and learn what it needed. He was to care for the garden. He was to guard it by keeping any harm or danger from invading it.

Adam was given responsibility over the garden. As one in authority he was held accountable for how he fulfilled his duties. Adam's decisions and actions would affect the condition of the garden:

> *"And unto Adam he said, Because thou hast hearkened unto the voice of thy wife, and hast eaten of the tree, of which I commanded thee, saying, Thou shall not eat of it: cursed is the ground for thy sake; in sorrow shalt thou eat of it all the days of thy life; Thorns also and thistles shall it bring forth to thee; and thou shalt eat the herb of the field;"*(Genesis 3:17-18)

"For the creature was made subject to vanity, not willingly, but by reason of him who hath subjected the same in hope,

Because the creature itself also shall be delivered from the bondage of corruption into the glorious liberty of the children of God.

For we know that the whole creation groaneth and travaileth in pain together until now." (Romans 8:20-22)

When Adam yielded to his wife's leadership that was contrary to God's command not only did Adam have consequences, but the creation did also. Adam's choice did not only affect him but that which was subject to him.

To be given a position of authority and leadership by God has never been, never is, and never will be a lighthearted task. It is not a place of lordship and domination, but a position of a servant.

"But Jesus called them unto him, and said, Ye know that the princes of the Gentiles exercise dominion over them, and they that are great exercise authority upon them. But it shall not be so among you: but whosoever will be great among you, let him be your minister, And whosoever will be chief among you, let him be your servant: Even as the Son of man came not to be ministered unto, but to minister, and to give his life a ransom for many." (Matthew 20:25-28)

In the Song of Solomon, Solomon likens the Shulamite woman whom the king is in love with to a garden.

"A garden inclosed is my sister, my spouse; a spring shut up, a fountain sealed. A fountain of gardens, a well of living waters, and streams from Lebanon.

Awake, O north wind; and come, thou south; blow upon my garden, that the spices thereof may flow out. Let my beloved come into his garden, and eat his pleasant fruits.

I am come into my garden, my sister, my spouse: I have gathered my myrrh with my spice; I have eaten my honeycomb with my honey; I have drunk my wine with my milk: eat, O friends; drink, yea, drink abundantly, O beloved." (Song of Solomon 4:12,15-16; 5:1)

Men, our wives are a lot like a garden. Just as Adam was given dominion over the Garden of Eden, God has given us dominion over our wife and home. He places us in authority over them.

1. Invest

    i. Plow (Dig) or Cultivate the Soil of her Heart

    Cultivating gets the ground soft.

        1. It takes time to get to know her

> *"Likewise ye husbands, dwell with them according to knowledge, giving honor to the wife, as unto the weaker vessel, and as being heirs together of the grace of life; that your prayers be not hindered."* (1 Peter 3:7)

           a. **Needs** (What are *her* needs?)
           b. **Weaknesses** (Where is she weak?)
           c. **Strengths** (What are her strengths?)

        2. Give honor to the wife: This prepares her heart to receive.

           a. Give outward respect; public displays of respect.

           b. Praise her – *"Give her of the fruit of her hands; and let her own works praise her in the gates."* (Proverbs 31:31)

    ii. Plant or Invest in the life of your wife

(You can't plant effectively until you have prepared the soil…which we did above.)

        1. Spiritual seeds

            a. Church
            b. Prayer
            c. Worship
            d. Bible study
            e. Tithing and giving

        2. Physical seeds

            a. Shelter
            b. Food
            c. Clothing

"But he that is married careth for the things that are of the world, how he may please his wife." (1 Corinthians 7:33)

        3. Emotional seeds

            a. Affection
            b. Compassion

This is where you can dig deeper and figure out which love language your wife has.

2.   Promote Growth

    i. Water the seeds that you have planted

        1. Encouragement

When you see growth in your wife's life encourage her in what you see. Point out the good things that are in her life.

ii. Fertilize: Enriching the soil (heart)

1. Prayer

"I have planted, Apollos watered; but God gave the increase." (1 Corinthians 3:6)

Only God can cause your wife to grow. You cannot make her grow. Pray for your wife. Pray that she will produce fruit that will glorify God. Pray for the seed that you have planted and watered to grow up in her. It is your investment that you have made into your wife.

iii. Weed: weeds choke out desirable plants

"He also that received seed among the thorns is he that heareth the word; and the care of this world, and the deceitfulness of riches, choke the word, and he becometh unfruitful."(Matthew 13:22)

As head of your wife and of your household, the man that God holds responsible for the leadership of your family, don't allow things in your lives that will choke out and hinder growth in you, your wife, and your children.

II. When it is not Easy

Our roles can be challenging enough when our spouse is doing everything right. There are times when we would say our spouse doesn't make it easy to do our part.

Example: A husband may say, "I know that I am to love and honor my wife but she is not loveable and the way she treats me makes it impossible for me to honor her. She nags me and she does let me lead our family because she thinks she is more spiritual than me. She doesn't respect me and the way she talks to me in public and in front of the kids embarrasses and belittles me. Does God expect me to do my part and fulfill my God given role and responsibility to my wife if she is not doing hers?"

Example: A wife may say, "My husband doesn't show me that he loves me. He doesn't honor me or even try to understand me. He ignores me and treats me rudely. My husband has lost my respect, he doesn't deserve for me to love him, serve him, or respect him. Does God expect me to do my part as a wife by respecting my husband and serving him when he is not doing his part in our marriage?"

Yes! He does. God is holding you responsible on judgment day for how you lived your life in light of your knowledge of his will for you. He will not sit you and your husband down together like a marriage counselor and let both of you plead your case of why you did not do what you knew to do. He will judge you alone for what you did and did not do. He will not say to you, "I know that your husband was hard to respect after all the things that he did to you. I know that you wanted to with all your heart, but he just made it impossible for you. I tell you what, your intentions were good and since he wasn't what he should have been to you this part of my word does not apply to you. Bless your heart my child."

Or…

"I know that your wife was contentious. She was a real hard woman to love and honor. She was disrespectful and thought that she was more spiritual than you were. She thought that she was better suited to lead your family than you were. Since she was so difficult I will not hold you accountable for not leading your family seriously and for not loving and honoring your wife. By the way I only meant for husbands to do that if they got a good wife."

"And whatsoever ye do in word or deed, do all in the name of the Lord Jesus, giving thanks to God and the Father by him…And whatsoever ye do, do it heartily, as to the Lord, and not unto men; Knowing that of the Lord ye shall receive the reward of the inheritance: for ye serve the Lord Christ. But he that doeth wrong shall receive for the wrong which he hath done: and there is no respect of persons." (Colossians 3:17, 23-25)

Chapter 5

God's Order – Wives

The Lord loves you and designed marriage to be a blessing and a wonderful thing. He has given us a manual for our marriages that gives us clear instruction. This manual is the Bible. God's Word is good for us and it helps us to know and understand our role in marriage. Marriage is designed by God and if anyone knows what it takes to have a wonderful marriage He does. Remember that we are not only to hear His Word but we are to apply it in our lives. The Bible says:

"But be ye doers of the word, and not hearers only, deceiving your own selves.
For if any be a hearer of the word, and not a doer, he is like unto a man beholding his natural face in a glass: For he beholdeth himself, and goeth his way, and straightway forgetteth what manner of man he was. But whoso looketh into the perfect law of liberty, and continueth therein, he being not a forgetful hearer, but a doer of the work, this man shall be blessed in his deed." (James 1:22-25)

Do you want to be blessed? Choose blessing over cursing by obeying the Word of the Lord.

Our first priority in our marriage should be the Lord; to love Him and please Him. The Bible teaches us that:

"He that hath my commandments, and keepeth them, he it is that loveth me…" (John 14:21)

Our demonstration to the Lord that we truly love Him is that we seek to obey the commands that He has given to us. God has given wives specific instructions in the Scripture that we will abide by if we love the Lord.

I.   God's Instruction for Wives

A. Submission:

"Submitting yourselves one to another in the fear of God. Wives, submit yourselves unto your own husbands, as unto the Lord. For the husband is the head of the wife, even as Christ is the head of the church: and he is the savior of the body. Therefore as the church is subject unto Christ, so let the wives be to their own husbands in everything." (Ephesians 5:21-24)

To submit means "to commit to the discretion or decision of another, yield, surrender, to put forward as an opinion."

When I read the word "yield" it makes me think of the road sign. You are driving along and come to the Yield sign and what are you supposed to do? Stop and look to make sure it is okay to keep going. Wives are to do that with their husbands. The wife should make sure it is okay with her husband before she takes a trip, spends a large amount of money, applies for a job, etc. Sometimes the husband can foresee things that the wife did not think about. Yielding is a way to keep the wife safe.

I (Brandi) remember my first lesson in submission. It happened when John and I were engaged. He was serving as a Youth Pastor at Mt. Yonah Baptist Church in Cleveland, Georgia. They were throwing us a wedding shower after church on this particular Sunday. I had spent the night in the girl's dorm at Truett McConnell University and I had packed two different church outfits to wear. One was a beautiful white flowing dress that came to my knees and it was sleeveless. It would look great with my tan. The other outfit was a peach button-down shirt that came to my elbows and up to my collar bone. I wore it with gray dress pants that fit loosely. I was going to wear the dress Sunday morning and to the wedding shower because it was dressier. John called me that morning as I was getting ready for church and he asked me, "What are you planning on wearing to church?" I answered, "Oh you know, that pretty white dress my Mom got me." He responded, "Well, did you bring anything else to wear to church?" I said, "Yes, I have a button-down shirt and pants." John said, "I'd like for you to wear that instead of the dress. I think the dress may draw too much attention to you."

I had a moment of decision where I could submit to him or do my own thing. I chose to submit to John even though we were engaged and not yet married. I respected him. He had been working at this church and he knew the people there and I did not want to disrespect them or him by wearing something flashy or inappropriate. When we got to church, we were sitting on the front left pew and the Pastor told us to open our Bibles to Ephesians 5. As I glanced down at my open Bible the words jumped off the page at me: *"Submit yourselves to your own husbands...in everything..."* (Ephesians 5:21-24) God taught me my first lesson in submission.

B. Reverence:

"This is a great mystery: but I speak concerning Christ and the church. Nevertheless let every one of you in particular so love his wife even as himself; and the wife see that she reverence her husband." (Ephesians 5:32-33)

The word reverence means "honor or respect felt or shown, a gesture of respect." It speaks of respect as being felt or shown. Our husbands can sense the attitude of our heart. They can feel disrespect or respect. Our husbands know by the tone of our voice, our attitude, and our body language whether or not we are respecting or disrespecting their leadership. We choose how we respond and react to our husband every day. We choose to respect him or disrespect him in the small things and the big things. The way we respond to our husband overtime can either build him into a greater man or tear him own.

Proverbs 18:21 says,

"Death and life are in the power of the tongue."

How we choose to speak to our husband can bring life or death to him. It also matters what we speak about him to others. Do not bad talk your husband to your children. That is disrespectful.

Again, you may be thinking, "Well my husband sure doesn't deserve my respect!" This is sometimes true, and this is why it is called a great mystery-when a wife can reverence her husband despite his behavior. It is not easy, but your rewards in this life and heaven will be great. Colossians chapter three speaks of setting your mind on things above and not on earthly things. When you are going through a hard time in your marriage, think about the Lord and about your eternal home in heaven. Think about your children and how your life affects theirs and generations to come. God does not say to respect your husband only if he is respectable. God does not say to submit to him only if he is a good spiritual leader.

"Likewise, ye wives, be in subjection to your own husbands; that, if any obey not the word, they also may without the word be won by the conversation of the wives;

While they behold your chaste conversation coupled with fear." (1 Peter 3:1-2)

The word *likewise* in 1 Peter 3:1 is telling wives to submit to their husbands even as Christ put himself under subjection and suffered at the hands of sinners. He did not say a word when they mistreated him. Christ submitted himself to serve sinners and we are to submit ourselves to serve imperfect husbands.

*"For what glory is it, if when you be buffeted for your faults, you shall take it patiently? **But if, when you do well, and suffer for it, you take it patiently, this is acceptable with God**. For even hereunto were you called: because Christ also suffered for us, leaving us an example, that you should follow his steps: who did no sin, neither was guile found in his mouth: who, when he was reviled, reviled not again; when he suffered, he threatened not; **but committed himself to him that judgeth righteously;** "* (1 Peter 2:20-23)

God is the judge on the throne, and he will judge your husband's misdeeds (if there be any). There are some cases like abuse that need to be dealt with differently. You need to seek help and get away from the situation, so you are not in danger.

II.   Challenges

"Marriage is not held on a romantic balcony, but on a spiritual battlefield." The Christian life is not easy. God's Word tells us we will have trials, temptations and difficulties. We seem to be willing to accept that and face the difficulties of life in most areas except marriage. People sometimes quickly divorce or check out emotionally to escape the difficulties of marriage. It is easy to think we should not have to work at marriage because it should come naturally. We base it on our **feelings** and emotions instead of His Word. We must be willing to work at our marriage. We must be willing to **examine** ourselves and see what we need to change instead of wishing our husband would change. Both husband and wife have things in their life that need to change in order to have a better marriage. Do not focus on whether or not your husband is doing his part. Instead, focus on yourself and ask God to show you where **you** need to change.

A. Our Husbands

God knows we aren't perfect and that we married an imperfect person. Some women may think they have married the wrong person and that someone else out there would be better, but everybody out there has their faults and problems. I have had seven different ladies tell me that they thought they married the wrong person. Well, once you are married it is too late to go back. You have to keep your vows and commitment to the one you married and make the best of it.

It is interesting to note the context of a verse on submission, which says:

"Wives, submit yourselves unto your own husbands, as it is fit in the Lord." (Colossians 3:18)

The verse right before it says:

*"And whatsoever ye do in word or deed, do **all** in the name of the Lord Jesus, giving thanks to God and the Father by him."* (Colossians 3:17)

We are pleasing the Lord when we operate in our role as a wife; loving, respecting and submitting to our husbands. We as wives will answer to God for our behavior as a wife and we cannot **blame** our husbands for why we did not do our part. Remember what the Lord did for us when we were undeserving.

"But God commendeth his love toward us, in that, while we were yet sinners, Christ died for us." (Romans 5:8)

We must die daily to ourselves. *"I am crucified with Christ: nevertheless I live; yet not I, but Christ liveth in me: and the life which I now live in the flesh I live by the faith of the Son of God, who loved me, and gave himself for me."* (Galatians 2:20)

Another challenge to submitting to our husbands is:

B. Sin

*Pride
*Rebellion
*Selfishness
*Insecurity
*Self-preservation

We think we are better or smarter than our husbands so we shouldn't have to submit to them. Sin tempts us to rebel against our husband and against God. Sin can cause selfishness to put a wedge in our marriage. We must put sin aside and humbly do what God desires. Sin goes both ways. If your husband is in sin and he is asking the family to make a decision that you do not agree with then you need to go to the Lord in prayer and ask God to speak to your husband. On two or three occasions I have disagreed with John about a big decision. I knew it would do no good to argue about it, so I prayed to God and asked the Lord to clearly and quickly speak to John about what to do and He did! Then John submitted himself to the Lord and moved in that direction.

C. Our Enemy

We have an enemy called Satan who wishes to destroy marriages and families and nations. He starts with the home, the marriage, and more specifically, he targets the **wife**. Look at Eve in the garden. Satan waited until Eve was created and he went after her.

"Now the serpent was more subtil than any beast of the field which the Lord God had made. And he said unto the woman, Yea, hath God said, Ye shall not eat of every tree of the garden?"(Genesis 3:1)

The enemy uses subtle things to attack us like music, movies, tv, radio, friends, family. Satan whispers lies that you almost don't notice.

In Genesis 2:17 God said not to eat of the tree of the knowledge of good and evil. You must know and look to the Bible. But Satan told Eve;

"For God doth know that in the day ye eat thereof, then your eyes shall be opened, and ye shall be as gods, knowing good and evil. And when the woman saw that the tree was good for food, and that it was pleasant to the eyes, and a tree to be desired to make one wise, she took of the fruit thereof, and did eat, and gave also unto her husband with her; and he did eat."(Genesis 3:5)

Eve followed her flesh in desiring the fruit. She fell for its beauty and followed her sensibilities instead of logic. **Eve wanted deeper spiritual insights than those provided by God.** We, like Eve, are easily deceived. Eve got caught up in her observation and opinion of it instead of looking to the Bible. This happens all the time and we as women sometimes don't realize it.

"For Adam was first formed, then Eve. And Adam was not deceived, but the woman being deceived was in the transgression." (1 Timothy 2:13-14)

Satan still uses the same strategy against women. Satan comes to us as an angel of light and seeks to deceive us when we least expect it. For example, the devil could use Christian radio or a professing Christian lady in your life to share with you things that sound spiritual, sound good, and make you feel good but do not line up with Scripture.

Here is an example: I was sharing with an older Christian woman about my struggle with a decision to quit a ministry outside the home or to continue in it. I told her that as I prayed about it the Lord spoke to my heart to focus on being a wife and a mother and a great peace filled my heart. As I talked with my husband about it, he told me that he desired my focus to be on my personal relationship with the Lord, my ministry to him as a husband, and my ministry to my children as a mother. He said I could still do that ministry as well (if my priorities were in that order) and left the decision up to me. The older woman told me if God was telling me to do something-for example, to teach a bible study-and my husband did not want me to, that I needed to tell my husband that I will always obey God above him and I should teach it anyway. At the time what she said sounded very spiritual and right. However, when I got home and thought and prayed about it, read God's Word, and shared it with my husband, I realized I had been deceived. Her counsel was contrary to Scripture. Scripture teaches wives:

" to love their children, to be discreet, chaste, keepers at home, good, obedient to their own husbands, that the word of God be not blasphemed."

Titus 2:5

But we, like Eve, think it is okay to "eat the apple" (or disobey God) even though God clearly says not to because we have been deceived into thinking it is right and good. Satan's goal is to deceive the wife, to get her to disobey God's Word and **begin leading her husband**. None of us are immune to deception. It happened to Eve. She took the fruit because she was deceived into disobeying God's Word, then she gave it to her husband. This caused the fall of man. Satan knows if he can get to us, we can get to our husband because one of their vulnerable spots is us. They will sometimes do anything for us, or to get us off their back! God gave our husbands to us to protect us and be our shield. They are not easily deceived. By their nature God made them more doubtful, skeptical, and factual than women. We as women are easily led by our senses and feelings. God made us this way so we could be mothers to our children, but we are not to come out from the shield of protection God made for us-our husband. God gives our husband wisdom and discernment as the head of the wife and the leader of the home.

God set up marriage in this way. When we stand behind our man, he can protect us. But when we get off on our own trying to be in control, our shield and covering is gone, and Satan comes in to deceive us.

III.   Fruit of fulfilling your role

A. Our Children

We as wives are a picture to our children of how the church should respond to Christ. You can leave a positive or negative impression on your children. If you share negative things about your husband to your children, they will grow up being mad or bitter toward you. Do not make your older children your marriage counselor or the person you vent to or ask for prayer from about your marriage problems. Find a trusted woman or counselor for that. The best way to make your children happy and secure is to have a good marriage.

"Her children arise up, and call her blessed; her husband also, and he praiseth her." (Proverbs 31:28)

B. Our Marriage

You reap what you sow. Sow good into your marriage and it will be blessed. It will suffer if we are not doing our part.

"Obey them that have the rule over you, and submit yourselves: for they watch for your souls, as they that must give account, that they may do it with joy, and not with grief: for that is unprofitable for you." (Hebrews 13:17)

Your husband has to give an account for your soul, so respect him for that and make it easy for him to love you and do his part with joy instead of grief. Wives who respect and submit to their husbands tend to have good marriages and wives who disrespect their husbands and think they know better than their husbands tend to have bad marriages. The wife may think she has a good marriage when in reality the husband is miserable but is pretending to be happy.

C. Our Testimony

"The aged women likewise, that they be in behaviour as becometh holiness, not false accusers, not given to much wine, teachers of good things; that they may teach the young women to be sober, to love their husbands, to love their children, to be discreet, chaste, keepers at home, good, obedient to their own husbands, that the word of God be not blasphemed." (Titus 2:3-5)

An unheard-of consequence for not submitting to, reverencing and obeying the scripture as a wife is that the word of God is blasphemed. Blaspheme means "irreverence for God, to speak evil of God". If we do not submit and reverence our husband as God has commanded us to in His Word, then we give the world an occasion to speak evil of our God. We are put on earth to glorify God not to cause his word to be blasphemed.

*"And David said unto Nathan, I have sinned against the Lord. And Nathan said unto David, The Lord also hath put away thy sin; thou shalt not die. Howbeit, because **by this deed thou hast given great occasion to the enemies of the Lord to blaspheme**, the child also that is born unto thee shall surely die."* (2 Samuel 12:13-14)

For God's namesake, His kingdom's sake and His glory let us obey His Word to us as wives.

Chapter 6

How to Protect our Marriages - Honesty

"Casting down imaginations, and every high thing that exalteth itself against the knowledge of God, and bringing into captivity every thought to the obedience of Christ;" (2 Corinthians 10:5)

I was asked a very interesting question while teaching a marriage workshop in the Philippines. One of the eldest women in the group asked what I would do if I saw a beautiful Filipino girl and thought that she would make a better wife for me than the one I had. This question caught me off guard because I wasn't expecting such a searching question. I responded with this question, "How many of you have ever had the thought that you married the wrong person and that someone else would be a better spouse for you?" To my surprise every person raised their hand without any hesitation. I remember thinking that if I were to ask that same question in a marriage workshop in America would there be any one that would have the courage to raise their hand? **Our culture has conditioned us to believe that it is better to look strong and be weak than it is to look weak and be strong.** We are fearful of what others may think if they really knew what we were thinking or what was in our heart. Somehow this mindset has crept into Christian marriages. We are not honest with our spouse about the struggles we have in our thoughts and imaginations. Because of this, marriages are being destroyed by adultery and other sins.

I shared with the marriage class in the Philippines a Scripture that gives clear instruction of how to handle thoughts and imaginations. This Scripture can be applied to many areas of life but for now we are going to focus our attention on protecting our marriages from adultery and ultimately divorce.

"Casting down imaginations, and every high thing that exalteth itself against the knowledge of God, and bringing into captivity every thought to the obedience of Christ:" (2 Corinthians 10:5)

I.   Shatter the Imagination

"Casting down imaginations"

Be very careful the things you daydream about. Satan is always looking for a way to destroy your marriage. If he can get to your marriage, then he has access to your children and grandchildren and also to your church family. He will attack through our imaginations. So stop those thoughts in their tracks!

II.   Shackle the Thought

"Captivity of every thought"

The battle ground is the mind. What we think about we eventually act upon. Don't allow ungodly thinking to remain in your brain. I heard it said once that it is impossible to keep a bird from flying over your head, but you can keep it from building a nest in your hair. Thoughts will fly through our minds, but we must not let them live there.

III.   Stand on the Truth

"Knowledge of God"

The battle is won or lost in the mind. If we do not deal with our thoughts and imaginations when they enter into our mind, we are in grave danger of falling and being defeated.

> *"Above all, taking the shield of faith wherewith ye shall be able to quench all the fiery darts of the wicked."* (Ephesians 6:16)

We have an enemy who shoots fiery darts at us. His target is the mind of the believer.

> *"In whom the god of this world hath blinded the minds of them which believe not, lest the light of the glorious gospel of*

Christ, who is the image of God, should shine unto them."(2 Corinthians 4:4)

While we are on this earth there will always be fiery darts. We cannot change that. It is what we do with the fiery darts that determines defeat or victory.

When thoughts and imaginations are left unattended in the mind, they have the potential to deceive us into forgetting who we are.

"Keep thy heart with all diligence for out of it are the issues of life." (Proverbs 4:23)

Before a man is born again his heart is dark and in union with sin (the spirit of error). As a result, he bears the fruit or the children of this inner union which are sins. After a man is born again, he is given a new spirit, the spirit of truth, the Spirit of Christ. This new spirit is clean, and it produces the fruit of the Spirit, which is all righteousness. As a new creature we know that we are sealed by the Holy Ghost of God and have been eternally redeemed, but the war rages against us from the outside now and this battle is won or lost with or without knowledge. We must guard our heart and keep evil and darkness from entering in. This is done by guarding our mind.

If we allow thoughts and imaginations that are against what we know about God to dwell in our minds eventually they will become products of the flesh. When a thought or imagination takes up residence in the mind it begins to grow roots. Eventually it sprouts and over time if it is left there it will bear bitter fruit after its own kind. We will eventually act on it and do the thing that we thought about or imagined. We must deal properly with every thought and imagination that is contrary to God's will concerning marriage.

Dealing with thoughts and imaginations that are clearly against the revealed will of God for marriage is the first step in protecting our marriage against adultery and divorce.

The second step is honesty with our spouse. Honesty is never wrong.

My wife and I set up accountability in our marriage to help protect us from adultery and divorce. One of those things is that we committed to be honest and tell each other if there was a person that was getting too close or a situation that could possibly set us up to fall into this sin of adultery.

For example, when we had only been married for a few years and had one little boy Brandi stayed at home with him while John went to work. She received monthly packages from a company that she ordered cleaning products from. The UPS guy was her age and he was cute. Brandi told John that the UPS guy that delivered packages was cute. John sat down and took Brandi by the hand and calmly prayed about the situation. The next delivery that came was made by a UPS man who was in his seventies. God fixed that!

We must remember that temptations are not sins.

"But every man is tempted, when he is drawn away of his own lust, and enticed.

Then when lust hath conceived, it bringeth forth sin: and sin, when it is finished, bringeth forth death." (James 1:14-15)

If we can learn to allow our spouse to be honest with us without being resentful and if we can learn to be honest with our spouse about temptations, we can protect our marriages from adultery and other sexual sin. When we confess our thoughts to God and to our spouse the plan of the enemy loses its power. However, if he can get us to keep little things from our spouse then he can eventually cause us to fall.

A good first step is to memorize 2 Corinthians 10:5 which says,

"Casting down imaginations, and every high thing that exalteth itself against the knowledge of God, and bringing into captivity every thought to the obedience of Christ;"

One of the best ways to stay out of sin is to memorize scripture.

"Wherewithal shall a young man cleanse his way? by taking heed thereto according to thy word.

With my whole heart have I sought thee: O let me not wander from thy commandments.

Thy word have I hid in mine heart, that I might not sin against thee."
(Psalm 119:9-11)

Marriage is under great attack in our world. No wonder since marriage is a key institution that communicates much about who God is and what He is like. Satan will stop at nothing to destroy every marriage. But remember:

[4] Ye are of God, little children, and have overcome them: because greater is he that is in you, than he that is in the world. I John 4:4

God is on your side and He is fighting for your marriage. We hope you will fight for you marriage. There are many lives counting on you. May God richly bless you and protect you as you make marriage last.

Made in the USA
Columbia, SC
08 February 2025

52874475R00036